Digging Up the Dead

DEATH RITUALS

By Sarah Machajewski

Gareth Stevens
PUBLISHING

Please visit our website, www.garethstevens.com. For a free color catalog of all our high-quality books, call toll free 1-800-542-2595 or fax 1-877-542-2596.

Library of Congress Cataloging-in-Publication Data

Machajewski, Sarah.
Death rituals / by Sarah Machajewski.
p. cm. – (Digging up the dead)
Includes index.
ISBN 978-1-4824-1274-1 (pbk.)
ISBN 978-1-4824-1228-4 (6-pack)
ISBN 978-1-4824-1484-4 (library binding)
1. Funeral rites and ceremonies – Juvenile literature. 2. Death – Cross-cultural studies – Juvenile literature. 3. Death – Social aspects – Juvenile literature. I. Machajewski, Sarah. II. Title.
GT3150.M33 2014
393–d23

First Edition

Published in 2015 by
Gareth Stevens Publishing
111 East 14th Street, Suite 349
New York, NY 10003

Copyright © 2015 Gareth Stevens Publishing

Designer: Andrea Davison-Bartolotta
Editor: Greg Roza

Photo credits: Cover, p. 1 Jones/Shimlock-Secret Sea Visions/Getty Images; cover, back cover, pp. 1–32 (background dirt texture) Kues/Shutterstock.com; pp. 4, 6, 8, 10, 13, 15, 17, 18, 21, 23, 24, 26, 29 (gravestone) jayfish/Shutterstock.com; p. 5 Mark Andrew Kirby/Lonely Planet Images/Getty Images; p. 7 (main) Zai Aragon/ Shutterstock.com; p. 7 (inset) Mark Yarchoan/Shutterstock.com; pp. 8, 9, 10–11 DeAgostini/Getty Images; p. 12 Federico Rostagno/Shutterstock.com; p. 13 Kenneth Garrett/National Geographic/Getty Images; p. 15 (bottom) Egyptian/The Bridgeman Art Library/Getty Images; p. 15 (top) BasPhoto/Shutterstock.com; p. 16 Werner Forman/Universal Images Group/Getty Images; pp. 16–17 Khaled Desouki/ AFP/Getty Images; p. 19 (top) Universal Education/Universal Images Group/Getty Images; p. 19 (bottom) Nutexzles/Shutterstock.com; pp. 20–21, 21 (top) China Photos/Getty Images; p. 23 Tim Graham/The Image Bank/Getty Images; p. 25 M R/ Shutterstock.com; p. 26 Richard Ellis/Getty Images; p. 27 John Block/Blend Images/ Getty Images; p. 28 Varghona/iStock/Thinkstock.

Printed in the United States of America

CPSIA compliance information: Batch #CS15GS: For further information contact Gareth Stevens, New York, New York at 1-800-542-2595.

CONTENTS

Words in the glossary appear in **bold** type
the first time they are used in the text.

A MATTER OF LIFE AND DEATH

Death is as old as life itself. From the earliest people who first roamed Earth's untouched lands to the people alive today, all **cultures** have treated death in their own unique way. Whether they were happy celebrations or **brutal** killing ceremonies, almost every culture developed **rituals** to deal with the dead.

Many death rituals may seem odd to us, but studying them teaches us much about how societies—both ancient and modern—viewed life. The death rituals discussed in this book are strange, fascinating, and definitely creepy. We'll go from ancient lands to our very own backyards on a quest to understand life as seen through the eyes of death. Along the way, we'll see how thousands of years of handling death have shaped our **customs** today.

GRAVE MATTERS

The earliest known human burial dates back about 100,000 years. Human remains were found buried with grave goods—including tools—in the Skhūl Cave near Mount Carmel, Israel. The tools' nearness to the remains suggests they were used in a ritual.

The scene here comes from a royal cremation ceremony in Thailand. Members of the royal family are believed to have come from heaven to rule and to return there after death. The elaborate structure built for a royal cremation represents heaven.

Where Does Death Take Us?

Ancient death rituals suggest a belief in an **afterlife**. In several cultures, the dead were equipped with food, water, and belongings that were supposed to help them after death. Modern rituals also reflect a belief in life after death. Most death rituals suggest that societies believe a person survives death in some way. That's where the rituals come in—they help the dead complete their journey to the world beyond.

THE MAYAN AFTERLIFE

The ancient Maya were Mesoamerican Indians who formed an empire in what is now Mexico, Guatemala, Belize, and Honduras that lasted from around 1800 BC until around AD 900. Scholars consider them to be one of the greatest ancient civilizations of the Western Hemisphere. They had a well-organized social structure, built pyramids and temples, and made impressive developments in mathematics and astronomy. They also had many death rituals.

The ancient Maya were very religious and believed their gods influenced every aspect of their lives. If the gods were happy, they would make things nice for the people on Earth. The death rituals were performed as a way of paying respect to the gods. The Maya also viewed their rituals as a way to ensure safe passage to the underworld, where they believed people went after they died.

GRAVE MATTERS

The positioning of graves was very important to the Maya. Bodies were buried facing the direction of the Mayan heavens, which is where the gods and special ancestors were believed to live. Graves were located in or around caves, which were thought to be entrances to the underworld.

Shown here are some of the ruins of the great Mayan city of Tikal in what is now Guatemala. Tikal began as a small village in the sixth century BC and had become a major ceremonial and trading center by AD 100.

A Civilization in Ruins

Mayan ruins weren't properly explored until the mid-1800s. As the sites were uncovered, explorers found ceremonial centers, temples, and caves. Most of these locations were covered in ceremonial art. Explorers also found evidence of the Mayan writing system. These discoveries revealed the ritualistic nature of Mayan religion, which was based on gods, the sun, the moon, rain, and corn. These beliefs helped shape Mayan death rituals.

Temple I, Tikal

7

All Mayan death rituals involved treating the body in a special way. However, treatment of a person's body depended on who they were in life. The civilization's most important rulers were buried in **lavish** tombs, while common people were likely buried where they lived.

The Mayan dead were laid to rest with objects that could help them on their journey to the underworld. Many were buried with a piece of corn, or maize, in their mouth. Maize **symbolized** rebirth. It was also meant to be food for the **deceased** on their journey. Mirrors were included to help the dead "see" the gods. Similarly, whistles were included to help the dead navigate their journey. In some cases, the deceased were buried with people who had been sacrificed to be their companions in the afterlife.

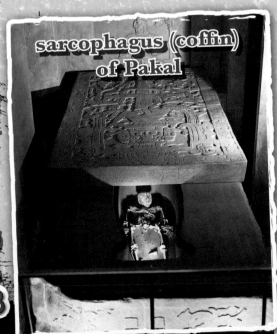

sarcophagus (coffin) of Pakal

GRAVE MATTERS

Pakal, a great Mayan king, spent 8 years preparing for his burial. He was buried wearing a death mask made of 340 pieces of jade, which was meant to show him at the height of his youth.

Pakal was buried deep inside the Temple of the Inscriptions at Palenque in what is today southern Mexico. The inside and outside of the temple are covered in hieroglyphics, or writing that looks like pictures, that narrate important Mayan events and the lineage of their rulers.

The Royal Court of Clay

In northern Guatemala, sometime around AD 600, a Mayan ruler was buried in a royal tomb accompanied by his entire court—or a clay version of it, at least. Archaeologists discovered 23 clay figurines that included a king, queen, priest, and other court members. The figurines may have been modeled to represent a court scene of conjuring, which was a ritual designed to send the soul of the dead ruler to his ancestors.

A PYRAMID OF DEATH

Nobody knows who founded Teotihuacán (tay-oh-tee-wah-KAHN). But whoever they were, they were brutal. Teotihuacán has two great pyramids called the Pyramid of the Sun and the Pyramid of the Moon. In the early 2000s, archaeologists uncovered piles of human remains, severed skulls, animal skeletons, and grave goods deep inside the Pyramid of the Moon—all evidence of **gruesome** ritual killings.

Scientists know the sacrificed people didn't go willingly. Some were found beheaded. Others had their hands tied behind their back. They may have been buried alive.

GRAVE MATTERS

Teotihuacán reached its height in AD 400 and was mysteriously abandoned around AD 600. The Aztec Indians discovered the ruins of the Pyramid of the Moon during the 1200s.

Archaeologists believe the sacrifices were performed to honor each stage of the pyramid's construction. But there may be another reason: human sacrifices showed a ruler's power. By seeing others' unlucky fate, people made sure to never disobey their leader.

The Aztecs guessed that the Pyramid of the Moon was a tomb. They called the street leading to it the Street of the Dead.

Deathly Symbols

Human remains weren't all that was found in the Pyramid of the Moon. The burial site includes many objects that were likely symbolic to the unknown society. Remains of animals that symbolized power—such as pumas, eagles, and wolves—accompanied the human skeletons inside the pyramid. Beads were found in the mouths of unearthed skulls. The gravesite also had figurines wearing necklaces and large earrings. Their meaning? Still unknown, just like much about this mysterious civilization.

ENDURING FOR ETERNITY

Throughout history, almost every culture's death rituals and customs have involved special ways of preparing a **corpse** for the afterlife. The most elaborate example of this was in ancient Egypt—think mummies, coffins, and pyramids.

The ancient Egyptian civilization formed around 3150 BC near the Nile River. At its height, ancient Egypt was an advanced society ruled by pharaohs and queens. Its death and burial rituals reflected its social order—the most important people in society were buried in the most expensive and lavish way. People in the lower classes followed similar funeral customs, but a less expensive version of them.

Ancient Egyptian burial customs were based on the belief that the physical body was needed in the afterlife. These beliefs motivated Egyptians to develop a complex way of preserving the dead.

mummy in coffin

A God Survives Death

In Egyptian mythology, the kind god Osiris was killed by his brother Seth, who wanted the throne for himself. Seth tore Osiris's body to pieces and scattered them around Egypt. Osiris's wife, Isis, recovered the pieces and put them back together. She then performed a spell that brought Osiris back from the dead. According to legend, Isis's spell was passed on to Egyptians, who used it to **resurrect** their own dead after they left the world of the living.

Osiris was often shown with green skin, as in this tomb painting. It was a sign of rebirth.

GRAVE MATTERS

Osiris's story shaped ancient Egyptians' ideas of death. They believed if they performed the rites and spells that resurrected Osiris, their own people would survive death, too.

Preparation for burial began at the time of death. Professional **embalmers** handled the body in a process that took about 40 days and ended with a mummy. The process began by washing the body with oils and water from the Nile River. Embalmers then removed the organs. This prevented the body from decaying on the inside. The organs were washed, dried, and put into jars, which were later buried with the body.

The next step was drying the body. Embalmers packed bags of natron (a mixture of salts) into the body to help dry it. They also packed it with sawdust, linen, and bandages to keep it from collapsing. When the body was thoroughly dry, embalmers coated it with waterproof materials and wrapped it in bandages. The embalming and mummification were then complete.

That's a Wrap

Wrapping the mummy was the final step in preparing the dead. Embalmers wrapped the body in strips of linen. As the body was wrapped, priests recited spells that protected the deceased and helped them journey to the afterlife. Embalmers placed small **amulets** in between the folds of the linen to ward off evil spirits. A papyrus scroll containing spells was placed with the body, too. Mummies were then placed inside coffins, where they waited until funeral processions began.

Anubis was the Egyptian god of embalming and mummification. In mythology, he weighed the heart of the deceased against a feather. If the heart was lighter, Anubis would lead the dead to Osiris.

GRAVE MATTERS

Embalmers removed the brain using a long hook they inserted through the nose. All other organs were removed and preserved except for the heart. It remained in the body because, to Egyptians, it was the center of intelligence and life.

Anubis

An Egyptian funeral began once the mummification process was complete. The family of the dead gathered to mourn the loss and honor the deceased's life. *Kites*, professional women mourners who sang burial songs, attended the funeral to loudly mourn the loss. Egyptians thought great grief at a funeral echoed in the afterlife. This helped the dead continue to exist there.

Open Wide

Before the body was laid to rest in the tomb, a priest performed a ritual called the "Opening of the Mouth" ceremony. The priest used special tools to touch the mouth, nose, and eyes of the deceased. They believed this restored the body's power to breathe, drink, and see. The ceremony was sometimes performed on statues, too. The ritual was a symbolic way of bringing a body back to life.

Following the funerary rituals, the body was placed inside a tomb. Some tombs were pits in the ground. But others—like the Great Pyramid—were tombs for pharaohs and queens. All dead were buried with valuable objects that would help them in the afterlife, such as food, drink, clothing, and furniture. The richest were buried with jewels, money, and other expensive objects.

Some ancient Egyptians were even buried with dolls, which represented the servants who would wait on them in the next world.

GRAVE MATTERS

In 1954, archaeologists discovered a boat in the Great Pyramid of Khufu. Some think it was intended to help the pharaoh sail the heavenly oceans forever.

DEATH—AN INTERRUPTION OF LIFE

The ancient Chinese believed that death was actually a continuation of life. They saw the process of dying as simply an interruption. Their death rituals, then, were a way to aid the dead in making a smooth journey to the afterlife.

Chinese rulers were often buried in complex tombs with objects to assist them after death. This included not only everyday items, but also fine metals and jewelry. Many tombs that housed the wealthiest people included jade, which is a precious stone that was thought to represent immortality. Rulers of the Han **dynasty** were even buried in jade suits. Once the dead were buried, the living made shrines in their honor. These were the sites of routine offerings that would keep the dead happy in the afterlife.

GRAVE MATTERS

The ancient Chinese felt that their ancestors could communicate with the gods to bring good fortune to the living. Giving the dead a proper burial ensured they'd be happy in the afterlife and therefore would bring favor to those left behind.

This ancient Chinese burial suit is made of jade tiles sewn together with gold thread.

Inside the Emperor's Tomb

In 1974, workers digging a well in Xi'an (SHEE-ahn), China, unearthed an incredible discovery: thousands of life-size clay soldiers, each with a different face, clothes, and weapons. The clay figures are part of the tomb of China's first emperor, Qin Shi Huang (CHIN SHEE HWAHNG), who ruled from 246 BC to 208 BC. The clay figures represented the army the emperor needed after he died. Experts estimate that there may be as many as 8,000 figures in the terra-cotta army of Qin's tomb.

Modern Chinese death rituals are different from those of the past, but their views of the afterlife are similar. While the dead are no longer buried in tombs, Chinese families still perform funerary rituals to help the soul reach its final destination.

Today, Chinese funeral customs are all about the living showing respect and loyalty to the dead. Following a death, the sons of the dead wash the body three times. Then, the body is clothed and placed inside a coffin. Important items are placed with the body. Then, a wake is held for about 3 days, and an overnight **vigil** is held on the final day. After that comes the funeral procession and burial. At the end of this ritual, the deceased is officially regarded as an ancestor.

During funerary rituals, families may burn joss incense, or they may include it as part of an ancestral offering at a later time.

Ghost Paper

The burning of joss paper and sticks is a defining feature of Chinese funerals. Joss paper is made of bamboo paper or rice paper and is dyed different colors based on the ceremony in which it's used. White joss paper, also known as "ghost paper," is burned at funerals, where it's folded, burned, and placed in a ceremonial pot. This is usually the last act at a Chinese funeral.

burning joss paper

GRAVE MATTERS

A band of musicians leads the procession of a traditional Chinese funeral. The loud music is meant to scare away evil spirits and ghosts that may hang around the funeral site.

21.

A FUNERAL PYRE FIRE

Some cultures' death rituals focus on getting rid of a body immediately in order to free a person's soul. Cremation, or burning, is one method. This ritual is commonly practiced in Hindu culture.

Hindu death rites begin when someone is near death. A Brahman, or priest, recites sacred texts over the person. Immediately after death, the relatives wash the body, dress it with clothes and jewels, and cover it with flowers. Mourners transport the body to a cremation site, which is usually along a river. There, the body is placed on a funeral **pyre**. More sacred texts and rites are recited. The oldest son then lights the pyre, and the cremation begins. This marks the beginning of the family's mourning period.

An Incendiary Custom

Imagine setting yourself on fire. You would never do that, right? Indian women once practiced suttee by throwing themselves on their husband's funeral pyre. This custom may have come from the myth about the Hindu goddess Sati, who burned herself to death to defend her husband's honor. It may also have begun because widows were the lowest people in Hindu society. Either way, this incendiary custom was outlawed in India in 1829.

Hindus believe in reincarnation, or the idea that the soul begins a new life in a new body after death. They believe cremation helps the soul quickly leave the body.

GRAVE MATTERS

The family of a deceased Hindu performs rites honoring the dead for at least a year. These *shraddha* are performed to nourish, protect, and support the spirit of the dead as the soul moves from one world to the next.

STRIPPED OF FLESH

Zoroastrianism (zawr-uh-WAHS-tree-uh-nih-zuhm) was founded in Persia (ancient Iran) and is still practiced by thousands of people around the word. Zoroastrian burial customs focus on properly disposing of a body so the soul can move on.

Geh sarnu, the Zoroastrian funeral ceremony, begins immediately after death. Priests recite prayers over the body. Relatives wash and dress the body in white cotton clothes. *Nasa-salars*, or pallbearers, handle the body while a priest recites prayers and reads the funerary rites. Halfway through the ceremony, a four-eyed dog (a dog with white spots of fur over his eyes) is brought in to confirm that the person really is dead. From there, the *nasa-salars* transport the body to a "tower of silence" where it awaits the last burial rite—being stripped of its flesh by birds.

GRAVE MATTERS

Zoroastrians believe a dead body is impure and will contaminate the earth if any of it stays around. Since cremation contaminates the air and burial contaminates the ground, their death rituals focus on getting rid of the body…completely.

To the Tower

Circular stone *dakhmas*, or towers of silence, may look innocent at first glance. But they're where dead bodies are laid out and exposed to the elements to be destroyed forever. On top of the tower, shielded by nothing, the flesh is eaten by vultures. This fulfills the belief that a body must not come into contact with fire or earth. The bones are either dumped in a pit or are moved and permanently kept in bone chambers called ossuaries (AH-shuh-wehr-eez).

DEATH—A HAPPY OCCASION

The Day of the Dead, or *Dia de los Muertos*, is a Mexican holiday that's been around for thousands of years. On this holiday, people honor their ancestors and invite their souls to return to pay a visit. The holiday teaches that death is a natural part of life—not something to be feared. Families celebrate by sharing funny stories, eating specially prepared food, and celebrating all night. They create altars to honor the dead and cover them with candles, flowers, pictures, and other possessions the dead enjoyed in life.

This holiday combines ancient and modern beliefs about death. The altar offerings reflect Catholic beliefs, while decorative skulls represent death and rebirth, just as they did for the Aztecs in ancient times.

GRAVE MATTERS

The Aztecs held a month-long festival to celebrate the death of their ancestors and honor Mictecacihuatl (meek-tay-kah-SEE-wah-tuhl), the queen of the underworld. Over thousands of years, this festival evolved into *Dia de los Muertos*.

Las Calacas

Skeletons may make you think of Halloween, but for cultures that celebrate *Dia de los Muertos*, they're much more than that. *Calacas*, as they're known in Spanish, are commonly used to decorate the altars and graves of loved ones during the holiday celebrations. They're also made into dolls, candies, and parade masks. *Calacas* are almost always shown dressed in fancy clothes and enjoying life. This is supposed to show that death is a joyous occasion, not something to be feared.

This photo shows an altar with *ofrendas*, or offerings, to the departed, including fruit, *calacas*, skulls, and *pan de muerto*, or bread of the dead.

DYING IN MODERN TIMES

Modern death customs may seem mild compared to those of the past. Today, a coroner must declare a person dead. A person is embalmed (though the methods are far different from those of ancient Egypt), and then a wake, funeral, burial, or cremation may follow. The rites and ceremonies associated with these acts depend on a person's religious beliefs.

Certain aspects of ancient burial customs can be seen in today's way of handling the dead. Practices ranging from the preparation of a body, to the prayers recited over it, to the rituals performed by the living after one dies are shared amongst people of all cultures, races, and religions. Death rituals vary from culture to culture and have greatly changed over time. However, there's one thing that unites them all—disposal of the dead has always been treated with special significance.

modern graveyard
with flowers

Shared Rituals

tombs
- ancient Maya
- ancient Egyptians
- ancient Chinese

burial with grave goods
- ancient Maya
- ancient Egyptians
- ancient Chinese
- Teotihuacán

offerings to the dead
- Chinese
- *Dia de los Muertos*

burial
- ancient Maya
- ancient Egyptians
- Chinese
- modern people

cremation
- Hindus
- modern people

priests recite prayers
- ancient Maya
- ancient Egyptians
- Hindus
- Chinese
- Zoroastrians
- Christians, Jews, Muslims

body is washed after death
- ancient Egyptians
- Chinese
- Hindus
- Zoroastrians
- modern people

Religious Traditions

The world's religions have their own unique death rituals. In Christian burials, the most solemn moment is the committal, or lowering of a casket into the ground. A priest usually recites the famous prayer that begins with "Ashes to ashes, dust to dust." At Jewish funerals, the immediate family tears a piece of their clothing right before a funeral begins to symbolize their loss. According to the beliefs of Islam, a deceased Muslim is buried facing Mecca, the Islamic holy city.

GRAVE MATTERS

In the United States, large, modern cemeteries didn't appear until 1830. Before that, the dead were buried in churchyards, town commons, or city graveyards.

GLOSSARY

afterlife: life after death

amulet: an item, often jewelry, thought to bring good luck or keep evil away

brutal: very violent

corpse: a dead body

culture: the customs, arts, social institutions, and achievements of a particular nation or group of people

custom: a traditional and widely accepted way of behaving or doing something that is specific to a society, place, or time

deceased: a dead person

dynasty: a family of leaders who rule a group or country over a long period of time

embalmer: one who embalms, or uses chemicals to preserve a corpse from decay

gruesome: gross and horrifying

lavish: rich, elaborate, or luxurious

pyre: a heap of burnable material, especially for burning a corpse as part of a funeral ceremony

resurrect: to bring back from the dead

ritual: a religious or solemn ceremony consisting of a series of actions performed according to tradition

symbolize: to stand in for something else

vigil: a period of keeping awake during a time usually spent asleep, usually to keep watch or pray

FOR MORE INFORMATION

Books

Noyes, Deborah. *Encyclopedia of the End: Mysterious Death in Fact, Fancy, Folklore, and More.* Boston, MA: Houghton Mifflin Company, 2008.

Sloan, Christopher. *Bury the Dead: Tombs, Corpses, Mummies, Skeletons & Rituals.* Washington, DC: National Geographic, 2002.

Websites

Egyptians
www.bbc.co.uk/history/ancient/egyptians/
The British Broadcasting Company provides a comprehensive look at ancient Egypt and its fascinating customs and rituals.

Your Family's Funeral Traditions
http://www.pbs.org/pov/homegoings/funeral-traditions.php#.
UzMRBV6Sc-1
PBS hosts an ongoing project where people contribute their own culture's funeral traditions.

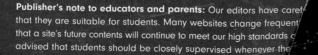

32

INDEX

INDEX